Praise for
The Ups and Downs of Living Alone in Later Life

"*The Ups and Downs of Living Alone in Later Life* is confident, lyrical, and unhurried— a wise woman reflecting on a meaningful life. Myrtle Stedman's openness and generosity, her close-to-the-bone honesty, are remarkable. She knows from whence she's come and where she's headed, and that she has further yet to go. After nearly a century, Stedman retains the wide-eyed wonder of innocence and the skill to impart it. Myrtle Stedman is one of the world's best arguments for honoring the wisdom of elders."

—Larry Dossey, M.D., author of *Reinventing Medicine* and *Healing Words*

"This is a book of great beauty and depth. It requires the experience of age to write such a book."

—Oren R. Lyons, Professor of American Studies, New York State University at Buffalo; Faithkeeper, Turtle Clan, Onondaga Nation; author of *Exiled in the Land of the Free*

"Myrtle Stedman's poetry poignantly reminds us that the flames of creativity and passion know no endpoint in the life cycle. In her tenth decade, she has written an epic poem, spanning the ups and downs, the depths and heights of human experience."

—Gene D. Cohen, M.D., Ph.D., Director, Center on Aging, Health & Humanities, The George Washington University; author of *The Creative Age*

"These poems are, indeed, very beautiful and will give people the joy of beauty, peace and plenitude."

—The Duchess of Bedford, author of *Nicole Nobody*

"Myrtle Stedman's intuitive yet profound poetry carries the varied messages of her ripe, agile and productive mind. In *The Ups and Downs of Living Alone in Later Life*, Stedman probes for psychological and religious meaning in late life and clings to her unique individual vision. No matter the experience, whether understanding herself, the land, or the spiritual and biological universe, her poetry unfolds in simple beauty."

—Dorothy Perron, Ph.D., gerontologist

"Myrtle Stedman illuminates the importance of the foibles of life, paying close attention to the moment. As she integrates religion and spirituality, her writing touches the soul. This book is for anyone who would make time for reflection, whether 15 or 100 years old."

—William A. Guillory, Ph.D., President and CEO, Innovations International; author of *The Living Organization—Spirituality in the Workplace*

"Growing old gratefully as well as gracefully, the forms in Myrtle Stedman's book are simple and spare, a lean and elegant architecture in this language. Her poems come as naturally and sturdily from her life as adobe does from earth. Reading these poems is so immediate, it's like having tea with this great elder, *Living Treasure*, and wise woman."

—Joan Logghe, National Endowment for the Arts fellowship (poetry); author of *Blessed Resistance* and *Sofia*

OTHER BOOKS BY MYRTLE STEDMAN

The Universal Mind Trilogy:
  Of Things To Come
  The Way Things Are Or Could Be
  Of One Mind

Ongoing Life

Artists in Adobe

A House Not Made With Hands

*Rural Architecture of Northern New Mexico
and Southern Colorado*

Adobe Architecture (with Wilfred Stedman)

Adobe Remodeling and Fireplaces

THE UPS AND DOWNS OF
LIVING ALONE
IN LATER LIFE

A New Look at Life by
Myrtle Stedman

SUNSTONE
PRESS

SANTA FE

Sunstone books may be purchased for educational, business, or sales promotional use. For
information please write: Special Markets Department, Sunstone Press, P.O. Box 2321,
Santa Fe, New Mexico 87504-2321.

FIRST EDITION

10 9 8 7 6 5 4 3 2 1

Library of Congress Cataloging-in-Publication Data:
Stedman, Myrtle.
    The ups and downs of living alone in later life: a new look at life / Myrtle
Stedman.— 1st ed.
       p. cm.
   ISBN: 0-86534-321-7
   1. Aged women—Poetry. 2. Solitude—Poetry. 3. Aging—Poetry. I. Title.

   PS3569.T33823 L58 2000
   811'.54—dc21   00-061226

Published by   SUNSTONE PRESS
                 Post Office Box 2321
                 Santa Fe, NM 87504-2321 / USA
                 (505) 988-4418 / orders only (800) 243-5644
                 FAX (505) 988-1025
                 www.sunstonepress.com

*"The Spiritual is Biological and
the Biological is Spiritual"*

CONTENTS

CHAPTER I
ONE DAY

ONE DAY

I had a hard time breathing,
   besides having a hard
      time seeing.

I thought, "I have to
   have someone
      living with me."

The phone rang.

A nice voice asked,
"Do you have a small
   studio house
      to rent at present?"

"No," I said,
   "I don't."

Then she asked,
   "Do you know
     of anyone
       who

Might need someone
   to live with
      them—

I am a homebody,
I am a good cook,
   I don't smoke,
   I don't drink and
      I don't date."

How fast can a prayer
   be answered or
     a need be filled?

She came and stayed with me—

All went smoothly
   for a few days

Her meals, gourmet.

Then fancy baskets appeared
   in the kitchen
      on my countertop.

A brand new dish rack
   in my sink replaced
     one I had used
      for years,

A carved St. Francis
   came out of a modest
      stance

And stood where I couldn't
   see anything
      but him.

The baskets swallowed
   small flowerpots
     and plants.

Then she plugged in
   a new telephone.
"A present," she said.
It had two-inch letters
   on a side panel.

I cried, "Take it away—
I don't need to be reminded
   I am going blind!

And take back the baskets,
And what have you done
    with my old dish rack?
I've had it ever since
    I've had the sink."

"There was no way
    I could clean it up,"
        she replied.

Then one day she was on
    a chair going after
        an old stringy
           hanging
              plant.

"What are you doing?"
    I shouted at her.

"I just forked up the dirt
    and am removing the
        dead leaves,"
        she said.

Couldn't she see the
    golden brown
        against my
           window pane?

Why does she think
    all has to be green?

And this and that
    she changed.

I became afraid to
    look.

She was putting on the
    teakettle and setting
        out my soup.

"I've got to tell you," I said,
    "you are taking over
        the place.

And I am not going
    to allow it."

She went out.

"To get an early paper
    and I'll not be back
        until later,"
        she said.

The day was Sunday—

"There is chicken and broccoli
    for your lunch

And fresh tomato soup
    for your dinner,
        peaches and cream
        for dessert."

She gave me a hug,
    said "Bless you,"
    and left.

I fretted and stewed—

God almighty—
    why couldn't
        she let things
           be?

Weeks went by
    with gourmet
        meals
            here or there.

But I had to replace
    her mattress
        and springs

For her back, she said.

Six times she tried
    to get me to
        buy a Queen-
            size bed.

"Stop bringing this up,"
    I said.

"When you are not here
    I have to have a King
        for great grand-
            children to pile in
                with parents.

This sooner or later
    during the night
        when they
            are here."

A King was ordered
    but before it came
        she threw out a
            string of red
                chiles.

I retrieved it from
    the garbage
        truck

And I hunted her up again.

"It's not going to work
    between you
        and me,"
            I said.

"Why?" she asked.
    "I replaced them
        with a clean
            new string."

"It's too short
    and too clean,

I am not a hypochondriac
    about dirt
        and dust
            as you are.

Sted, my husband,
    once knew a sculptor
        who wouldn't
        allow his
            sculpture

To be dusted—
    'dust brings out the planes,'
        he said."

"You are a character,"
    she said over
        tears and
            laughter.

"There are not many
    left."

And she gave me a
   lipstick kiss
      and wiped
         my cheek.

"You are a character,"
   I said,

And gave her a hug
   and again
      she took off
         for the day.

Suddenly I became quiet
   and then began
      to laugh.

I had put my finger
   on why I was
      mad.

The old dish rack
   wasn't dirty

It was just yellow
   with age
      and memories

Of Thanksgiving
   dishes washed
      clean and
         shiny

And Christmases
   many

Of family conversations
   and of friends
      galore.

It heard Nell tell me one day,

"Stop caressing those
   dishes in the sink
      and get them
         in the rack.

I am standing here
   just holding
      the
         towel."

Oh how many times
   it just witnessed
      my unwinding
         after friends
            left.

I meditated in my own
   style over the
      situation.

I thought of the "One Day"
   which started
      my story

And gave thanks
   for the good
      her coming

Brought to the
   place.

SUCH AS

Gourmet meals
    of course

But a new mattress?

"How long have you had
    this mattress?" she
    had asked

The second morning
    she was here.

"You are supposed to
    get new ones
        every fifteen
            years."

The plants thrived on her
    attention

And she did all of the
    running around
        and shopping.

But besides the things
    we had need of

She never came home
    without a flowering
        plant or bouquet,

A new blanket
    when I had plenty
        and more than
            I need.

And one day new spreads
    for my beds—

"To replace your old
    faded ones," she said.

"Take them back," I said,
    flinging them
        aside,

"I like my old faded
    ones."

She had notions—
And insistence for
    what paintings I
        should take down

And which ones I should put in
    their place.

"They are my paintings
    and they are
        where
            I want them to be."

"I am thinking of you," she said,
    when she brought in
        a new tape recorder
        to put by my
            bed.

I had a good one in
    my study with
        an easy chair to
        sit in while
            listening.

OR SHE WAS ALWAYS
WAITING

"I don't need duplicates,
 I have too many
  things as it is,

So don't keep bringing
 things in."

"You need to learn
 to be more receptive
  and more polite,"
   she said.

And left again—

She was always
 going out.

For my driver to appear
 to move something
  or other

In her end of the
 house.

My driver took
 occasion, he told
  me,

To tell her to get along
 with me.

I didn't ask him
 what he said.

IN THE MEANTIME

What do I do?

If I wanted to change
      her

It would be no better
      than her wanting
          to change me.

So what do I do?

I am wasting a lot of
      time

Going over the situation
      again and again

Getting nowhere.

"IT'S A POWER STRUGGLE," SHE SAID

Whose power struggle—
   hers to take over
      and run my house

Or mine to maintain
   its integrity?

I always wondered
   what it would
      be like

For an independent person
   to call for
      help.

I am now first hand
   finding
      out.

I say, "Please don't
   do that,"

And that is exactly
   what she
      does do.

And when I quietly right it,
   fully expecting her
      to notice,

She does it again.
Again, I right it,

She does it again.
And I finally fly into
   a rage.

Is she stupid,
Or am I?

I really wanted to
   know

And am finding
   out.

She says, "You are a
   devil,"

And I agree
   and under
      my breath

I say, "Watch out."

This is a lot like
   being married
      again, like

Living with one who too
   owns the house.

REACHING OUT

She is reaching out and
    petting me as we
        pass by in the
          house this
            morning.

She can't say,
    "I am sorry,

I really love your
    house."

I finally did say
    such to Sted.

Sometimes he drew
    himself up and
        away

Sometimes he folded
    me up in his
        arms,
            thank God.

SHE IS GONE

As of two
    weeks ago.

But she called
    again.

"Do you think we
    could renegotiate?"
        she asked.

"Why do you want
    to come back?"

"Well, it's better the devil
    you know than
        the devil you
          don't.

I know you and
    you know me."

"I'll have to sleep on it,"
    I said.

But in the morning
    I knew it was,
        "No."

"You left me in
    a pinch

And called me
    a mean old
        woman.

So be it."

AFTER SHE WAS GONE

I went to the refrigerator
   to find what I could
      to eat.

Ah, a bowl of stewed pears
   and a Sara Lee
      sponge cake.

I wiped off a spot
   of orange juice
      from the cutting
         board

With an expandable
   sponge she kept
      by the sink,

And cut myself a piece
   of cake.

When I got to the table
   I had the sponge
      (right in color
         and shape)

But it was not
   the cake.

A QUIET MELLOWNESS

There is a quiet mellowness
   in a house which
      is not spotlessly
         clean.

There is a sense of
   peace where
      there is no fussiness.

A sense of peace
   which can be felt
      by a perfect stranger
         entering the house.

A quietness
   resides in a painting
      on a wall

And silence
   says it all.

Until it is time
   for something
      else

To be heard.

CHAPTER II
MELANCHOLY TURNED TO JOY

THIS DAY

Began as a melancholy
    day to the point of
        manic depression.

Never have I felt so
    melancholy—

So alone—so here
    when I wanted to
        be there—

With Sted; no, it was
    him with me I
        wanted.

This, the impossible—
    or so it is
        thought,

Yet, I could feel his arms
    about me—
        mine tightly
            hugging
                him.

Hallucinations—delusion—

He is burned up

Nothing left but his
    spirit,

But that is all there
    is.

Even of me—
    embodied
        still

So why do I feel
    depressed?

My spirit embodies
    itself.

He must want to be
    with me

As he did when he
    met with
        me

Even before, when
    he was only
        lonely

Thinking of such as
    me.

So why not now
    embodied
        to fit my need.

As I surely fit his
    long ago
        and for twenty-
            two years night
                and day.

And if Spirit
    is the Mind
        at work

Communicating,
    creating forms
        of life

Why not now
    just to let me
        know that

He still is.

A yogi can die,
    be buried

And, in the morning,
    be seen going
        about his usual
           thing;

Or call on a grieving
    student to
        declare that

He is in flesh
    and blood,
        then

Disappear as
    though he hadn't
        been there

Leaving the student
    absolutely convinced

That what he had
    experienced was
        real.

And other cultures
    have things to
        tell

That blow apart
    the closed
        mind.

Spirit of a necessity
    comes in two parts
        that they may
           work together

To form anything.

Forget the embodiment
    if we are thinking
        of people alone.

Everything is an embodiment
    of Spirit.

And it comes in pairs
    to make
        the whole.

24

I WENT BACK

To bed this morning—

I had given up thinking
    and just gave
        up to rest—

Instead I was
    restless and
        thought—

I want to break
    out of a
        stagnant
            period—

When I heard a
    very small
        voice ask,

"You want to open
    up?"

And I realized,
    "Yes."

And I saw a gate
    open two
        ways

From a post in
    the middle

And I got this feeling—

That as I open up
    something can
        come in—

And I was joyous,
    "Yes, yes."

There is so much
    that I want to
        know

Which I feel has
    been shut
        off

From my everyday
    living

That in knowing
    would add so
        much to my
            life.

Something growing
    out of the past

Which has always
    been a possibility

A potential for
    moving on—

An interest

A question waiting
    to be asked.

Or something
    undone

Waiting to be
    done.

THE SCIENTISTS TELL US

That energy and matter
   are interchangeable

And we know
   that Spirit is
      the Mind at work

Doing whatever
   it is of a mind
      to do—

Making love
   or a footstool—

Materializing ideas
   of the Mind.

So why should Spirit
   be such a mystery

And Materiality looked
   down upon?

I SAW MY DEPRESSION

Filled to the
    brim with joy

As an image on my
    drafting board.

And I saw that
    making things
        in the Mind's

Own image is the
    living process

As ideas to be
    conceptualized

By the Mind as the
    basic male and
        female—

From which all proceed.

As I lay there awake
    I could think of
        nothing that

Didn't go through
    this two way gate.

SO WE WERE AND ARE

Male and Female;

Spirituality in the
    raw

Making copies
    of ourselves

Like the waves
    on a pond.

Expressive and receptive
    conceptualizing
        form.

I laugh when
    Sted announces
        his presence

With a puff of
    Camel's cigarette
        smoke.

I WAS SO LITTLE

That my feet
   hung

Half way between
   my chair
      and the floor

When I made up
   my mind
      that

There were a lot
   of things between
      the school

And the church
   that had to be
      put straight

To get at the truth.

This has been in
   the back of my
      mind

Until now I am
   ninety and two;

And have come
   to make the
      postulate

That the spiritual
   is biological

And the biological
   is spiritual.

And I write
   from my own
      experience,

Welling up intuitively
   from deeply stored
      memories

Of conclusions
   stashed away
      in my genes

Since the day before
   I set foot out
      of the bog,

Or observed the
   things that
      were created

By the Spirit which
   moved everything
      to come forth

And do their own
   thing among
      all other
         things

Doing their own thing,
   learning to keep out
      of other things'
         way.

So I figured there
   was thinking
      and learning

From the very beginning,
and a certain amount
of Difference of
opinions.

But there was one
thing that we
all agreed about:

That we wanted to live.

And we instinctively
had from the
beginning

Made copies of
ourselves
by a

Division of Mind—

You do this and I'll
do the other

And we will both have
fun and enjoy
it.

And live forever
in copy after
copy of ourselves
making

Improvements as
we see fit along
the way.

So I saw this split
of Mind as
male and
female

Thus biological,
driven by a creative
Spirit

Which has brought
us to this day.

And I am sure
this is why we can
if we want

Call this Spirit
God because

Nothing would
ever have
been without
it.

CHAPTER III
WHEN I WAS A CHILD

AT HOME

I had a room
    all to myself.

It had one window
    with a gardenia
        bush outside.

It flowered heavily
    with an aroma
        which filled
            my room

And the house.

At night, the moonlight
    shone on the
        white flowers

And beyond
    over a garden
        and two sycamore
            trees, a quiet
                road,

A bridge,
    and a woodland.

I knelt at
    the window

And looked out
    at the world

And the heaven
    above.

I never could
    picture the Father
        up there

That Jesus always
    looked up to.

My father had a
    razor strop—

But never mind
    that.

I felt I knew
    Jesus personally.

I had an apple box
    that I set
        on end,

Covered with a
    scarf and
        a candle
            in a holder.

And I promised Him
    that I would
        work for Him
            every minute
                of my life.

And I felt the
    magnitude
        of what
            that meant.

His whole life
was spent
in healing

The broken Spirit
in all that had
materialized.

This is all that
is needed
now;

Which leaves nothing
wrong with the
materialization
of Spirit.

And in this Spirit,
or the movement
in the heavens,

A wedding between
the astronomers and
astrologers could
help us to see

The Father and now
Mother of all
life and invention

In this day
and age in a
meaningful
way,

As Universal
and Cosmic
Mind.

I WAS IN ADOLESCENCE

When I began to
read the Bible
on my own;

One thing I read
was, "Adam
knew Eve,

And Eve knew
Adam . . ."

I don't remember
what came
before or

What came after.

But when I wrote
the first book
of my trilogy

That statement
took on a very
clear meaning.

Where the knowing
had to do with
the Mind.

I think I had a
premonition
that some day

I would write
those books.

MAYBE I GOT MORE

From my dad
　　than I gave
　　　　him credit
　　　　　for.

He irked me for
　　being flirtatious
　　　　with

Other women
　　until past his
　　　　eightieth birthday.

But now I know
　　that it was
　　　　because

My mother was
　　cold to sex.

Sex was a bad
　　word in
　　　　my household,

Or their household
　　I should
　　　　say.

And it has taken
　　my own

To put it straight.

I have both
their ways
of thinking.

There is more to
sex than
we think.

It relates to the
basic balance
of the

Expressive and receptive
Mind.

My mother gave
birth to six
children

But her mind was
not bogged
down by
us.

It was always
lifted up to
creative ideas.

My father was a
builder;

His mind was ever
on physical
structure;

I inherited both
and that is
what I am

Writing about—
both—

Ideas and
structure.

THE ORDER OF ACTION

Of the Mind is
    fixed to

Work in a harmonious
    fashion objectifying
      Creation as

Created on an
    evolutionary track.

As long as it stays
    on this evolutionary
      track

All goes well.

When something is
    objectified that is
      off track

The machinery of the
    Mind is interfered
      with

And brings the work
    to a stand still:
      death.

The Mind can
    right Itself,
      bringing back

Its objectified Self
    to "on track,"

To a renewal
    of life or condition.

The form is not permanent,
    only the action
      of the Mind
        is permanent.

The action started, let us say,
    with Einstein's Big Bang.

The Mind and its
    consciousness of
      Itself

Never dies, or hasn't
    so far as is known
      to us.

And, if it does, we won't
    be here to
      notice.

BUT NEVER MIND

A lot of the fathers
   these days pay
      so little attention

To what is right
   and wrong
      in the same

Way we used to think
   of right and
      wrong

That we need a new
   image of Jesus'
      Father in heaven.

That image, not as a
   human father
      with himself only
         to decide what
            is right or
               wrong,

But as a planetary
   or cosmic expressive
      energy

Which engages a
   receptive energy
      and produces

An unconditional
   rightness far
      better than any
         personal God
            or father

Would be able to
   do.

IF THE SEEDS OF LIFE

Were scattered with the
    first Big Bang,

We are of the same
        stuff as the universe
            and are replicas

As waves of sound.
        And, in the replicas,
            are the seeds

Of the first, unchanged,
        making all heirs
            to the Father
                in heaven

Of all life on earth
        with the built-in
            capacity

For growth and
        expansion
            in harmony

With the whole
        universe.

This is why, if things
        get out of order
            or are poorly conceived,

We have to refer back
        to the seed, back
            to the Father

For reference of how
   things should be.

It is just like
   fixing a clock

We have to know
   how it was
      designed to
         run.

In other words,
   what did our
      slice of the
         explosion

Contain?

What was in it,
   as seed for
      our being,

Which is as fertile
   now as it was
      in the beginning,

And requires no
   time to be born
      of the Mind,

And leaves us
   to carry on
      what it started?

It is the
   idea and its
      construction—

Plan and the actual
   building, in architectural
      terms.

Energy and matter
   are interchangeable
      which only means

That we are only
   capable of seeing
      one

But not the other
   phase of the same
      thing at the same
      time.

MY MOTHER TOOK

The Farmer's Almanac
 and that,

I think, put a smoldering
 in my mind that
  has

Burst forth into the
 flame that is
  in my writing,

Casting reflections
 everywhere
  for

Better days and
 understanding.

It only makes sense
 to me now
  that Jesus

Would lift his eyes
 up to a Father
  in heaven.

And I never forget
 that the three Wise Men
  who followed the

Star over Bethlehem
 were astrologers
  who knew that

Such as Jesus
 should appear.

Or we probably never
 would have known
  about His work
   for other men—

And civilization.

There is no doubt
 about it.

We are all sons
 and daughters

Of His Father in
 heaven;

Each an essence
 of the Cosmic
  Life.

ONE TIME

My husband
    said, "There is
        one thing a man
            can't do;

He can't make
    man."

I said, "Oh, but he
    can—it is the
        easiest thing

He can do."

"How do you figure
    that?" he asked.

I said, "He loves!"

I HEARD A GROWN MAN

Say one time at
    a consciousness
        conference,

"I never have figured
    out what I am
        supposed to do

Or why I was put
    here."

He never made a
    commitment
        before he was born,

Or when he was
    a child, or

When he became grown.

Maybe his parents
    before him

Didn't do anything
    towards him
        but love.

I forgot about
    my commitment
        but it was
            made

In love

And that took care
    of its production.

AND ABOUT ASTROLOGY

One time my husband
    came into our
        bedroom

To get some change
    from a pocket
        in his pants

Hanging in the
    closet.

I was sprawled
    across the bed
        reading
            the

Horoscope for his
    birthday month.

He said, "Reading
    your funnybooks,
        I see."

"Listen," I said, "to
    what it says
        about you."

He never again
    referred to my
        funnybooks.

Because what I
    read described
        his very best
            nature

To a "t."

CHAPTER IV
FEET ON THE GROUND

WHAT NOW?

Has the universe
    to tell me

Now that I know
    that the Mind

Is both male and
    female;

What is there to
    know beyond
      this,

What is in this
    knowing?

It sounds too simple
    to ask

Yet I hear the
    scientists telling
      us

That all that exists
    is the manifestations
      of these two.

They make of themselves
    what we know
      of

As the material world.

"THE EARTH

Is the Lord's
    and the fruit
      thereof."

We are fragments
    of the Big Bang

Not lost out there
    but captured
      and retained

The ingredients of
    the universe—

The hologram.

THE IMMACULATE CONCEPTION

I told my son,
    "For three years
        I've been seeing
            through a
                fog.

Are the skies as blue
    to you as they
        have always
            been, in New Mexico?"

"Mom," he said,
    "They are as clear
        and blue
            as they have
                always
                    been."

I accepted his words
    and now I see
        them as they
            are,

And breathe
    with ease.

AT ONE POINT

I asked my doctor
    or I told him,

"I don't know why my
    hand is shaking."

And he said, "It's your
    uncertainty; you
      don't know
        what is going
          to happen."

I hadn't thought
    of it that
      way.

But when he had
    diagnosed what
      he had decided
        was wrong
          with me,

He had said, "Very serious,"
    and he had said
      it twice.

I didn't believe it,
    but I was shaking.

Ten years later I had
    another bout.

This is now and
    I am shaking.

I am not well
    and I am not
      sick.

I want to know
    which way
      am I going.

I have a lot
    to live for.

Is it important
    or should I just
      say, "Oh well?"

It is like standing
    at the edge of
      a precipice

It is also like
    turning back

To first find out
    where and why
      I feel like I

Should know
    where I am
      going.

I never have been
    without a map
      before.

That is why I feel
like turning
back

To draw that map
of a surety that
I and others

Can feel safe
to follow.

Now I have turned
back and I've
lost my shakiness

Within this hour.

WEEKS AGO

I said goodbye
    to melancholy

And buried it,
    but its ghost is
      back today

As alive as ever—

So as an Aquarian
    I have to deal
      with it again.

It takes me to the
    seamy side
      of life

Clear to the basement
    to look at all the
      stuff stored
        there.

It's a mess—

"Clean it out," it says,

"There is joy ahead
    so where will
      you put it

If you don't have
    room
      upstairs?"

So I dig in and soon
    am enjoying it

With thanks to the ghost
    of melancholy,

That rose up from the dead today.

I AWOKE AT 92

From an afternoon
    nap,

Sat up and looked
    at the mountains.

They were swathed
    in the dark blue
        of a heavy
            shower.

Lightning streaked
    down from the
        sky

Just as it did when
    we were at
        camp

And I looked from
    the flap of our
        tent as

I sat before my
    easel.

A cool breeze came
    in through
        the door

Bringing the fragrance
    of rain

And memory that
    sufficed for
        being at camp
            now.

IN GRATITUDE

For the snow.

You heard our
　　cry for snow

Above the expectations
　　for a sunny day.

Along with my
　　yearning for
　　　　snow or rain

I implored You
　　to think and
　　　　hear

Of the thirst in
　　the grass
　　　　and trees,

The waiting buds
　　of Spring:

They are all Yours.

I am glad You
　　heard our
　　　　call

For snow.

Its beauty is now
　　covering
　　　　everything

And even the weeds
　　are happy.

And the ones
　　who wanted
　　　　sun

Can have it now
　　for it is shining
　　　　on everything

And the roof tops
　　are dripping
　　　　and melting

The snow,

Giving the ground
　　the drink

It has been yearning
　　and gasping for—
　　　　too long!

Trees and grasses
　　only burn

When we forget
　　to be grateful

For the fact that
　　we are all
　　　　of the

Same stuff
　　and one.

THE WORD OF MIND

Is like the breaking
   of the waves,

Speaking of coming
   forward—

Turning back,
   gathering together
     and turning
      loose.

Then slowly
   moving, in
     an undertow.

If one is lying
   in bed

The movement
   can be felt

Coming through
   under the instep
     toward the heel
      of the foot.

Up through the legs,
   through the calf
     and the underside
      of thigh;

Into chakras
   one, two, three
     and four—

Five, six and seven
   and out;

In a never-ending,
   ever-present
     refrain,

The Mind never
   sleeping

It goes backward and
   forwards,

Fulfilling Itself
   in dreams,

Dying, only to give
   birth

And to further
   awakening

In a whisper or
   a cry.

Or I should have
   said this in
     reverse—

The waves and everything
   else

Reiterates whatever
   the Mind has
     in mind.

THERE ARE TIMES WHEN

Circumstances are no
  good.

We can go along
  with them
    as "no good;"

Talk about bad times
  and blame it
    all on circum-
      stances

Which prove you
  right by remaining
    "no good."

Until you can think
  of nothing else
    but "no good;"

And cry out, "My God,
  My God, why have
    you forsaken me?"

Which only drives
  the circumstances
    to the hilt,

Until you or I say,
  "Stop it."

We are putting the cause
  out there.

And "out there"
  may not
    care

Or is just going
  along with
    what is
      expected.

And somebody
  needs to take
    over

By calling the shots.

We are every one
  creative;

Every one is responsible
  for what goes on.

By what we think
  and do about
    it.

"In the day that
  you see both
    good and
      evil

Ye shall surely
  die."

I just had to throw
  that in.

IF YOU WERE TO ASK ME

What do I want,

I might give you
      a superficial
            reply;

Incomplete and
      very general.

That I don't
      usually get.

And, if I do, it is
      just as super-
            ficial,

Unsatisfactory,
      a temporary and
            sometimes a

Very trying thing.

But if I really
      have a very
            deep feeling

For what I want
      I may have to
            hold out

A long, long time
      wondering all the
            way, why?

I have come to the
      conclusion

That it is my sub-
      conscious
            holding out

For the real thing
      that I want

Just waiting for
      me to realize
            what it is;

To be specific
      and that pays
            off,

And very quickly the
      subconscious
            is

Bride to the conscious
      and what I really
            want is born.

TODAY THERE IS

No seal of agreement—
    no wedding
        ring.

This is a whole
    new thing

For us to deal
    with.

We have become
    like the animals
        of the earth.

More natural.

Where the children
    learn quickly

To take care of
    themselves

And where non-parents
    are involved
        for the good
            of all.

Yet every man
    can be seen as

The son of God,
    and every woman

The bride of Christ,
    if you are Christian.

I WAS BROKE

Money became
    my God,

I could think of
    nothing else,

But I was thinking
    of money
        as money

Not as God.

But if God is all
    in all

Then money is
    God

In the sense that
    God is everything:

Its value and substance
    with no limitation,

And I saw myself
    as having all
        I need.

This then became
    my obsession

And my spirit
    became uplifted

Instead of being
    depressed.

IS IT GOOD

To wonder, "What is for
   tomorrow?"

Or would tomorrow
   be "sufficient
      unto itself?"

Should we "take no
   thought of what
     we should
       eat

What we should
   put on to
     wear,

Or what we should say?"

Can we count on the
   "word being put
      into our mouth"

Leaving us carefree
   for today?

Why not?

The Mind is present
   at all times—

As good tomorrow
   as today—

Better because
   it will be right
      in the situation

That today has
   put us in.

Today is what we need
   to think about.

WITH THE MIND

At our disposal
   that knows
      everything

There is to know,

Why is it that we
   still grumble?

It is because we
   are not conscious

That It is here and
   there.

"An ever-present
   help in time of
      trouble."

The grumble is
   an important
      part of

Opening up.

It precedes the opening
   that will let the
      knowing in,

When we let go
   and let it
      come.

THERE IS ESTHESIS

In the meeting
   of minds

That brings on
   smiles

And new life
   when there
      was none.

EVERY SEED

Doesn't make
   a plant or
     a child.

The seed has to be
   conceived or
     conceptualized,

To find ground,
   acceptance,
     faith or fear,

To mature or not.

It is the same with
   an idea, a
     desire,

Or a prayer
   or again fear.

Has the thought
   or idea been
     taken in

Or cast off,
   found unaccepting
     ground

Or no ground
   at all for
     being?

WE HAVE A SPRING TIME

Of renewal
    just like the
        trees, grasses
           and flowers,

But our springtime
    of renewal
        is constant.

That is why we
    don't see
        our connections

To the flowers
    and all the
        rest of
           nature.

Everything else has a
    time for
        mating.

We mate whenever
    we choose.

What can that
    tell us but
        that

Mating is a process
    of Mind

And makes us realize
    that Mind and
        mating

Is for more than
    population,

It is for the making
    of all creation

And a thing unto
    Itself.

Never without
    a mate for
        mating;

Never having to
    seek,

Because Mind is
    fully replete;

It talks to Itself.

It is Itself's best
    mate.

All fascination
    and joy.

Is there to
    beget

Whatever it can
    imagine.

Our wholeness
    is in this
        image;

A companionship
    of wisdom
        and
            understanding.

CHAPTER V
I DON'T NEED TO GO ANYWHERE

I AM OVERWHELMED

With the beauty
   of the earth

The beauty around
   me

That I call mine—

My home
   with an open
     field in front

Is flooded with the early
   morning sun—

Magnificent trees
   in back
     and to the sides.

A paradise
   and mine.

I cry with joy
   and appreciation

For such a good
   life.

I know that there
   are beautiful
     places

All over the planet

And people who love
   them just
     as I.

I DON'T NEED TO
GO ANYWHERE

I have an ongoing
    romance

With life itself
    right here
        in my
            house,

In all my experiences
    and my
        imagination.

I can fix up things
    that I couldn't
        before by going

Through the experience
    now as then.

I HAVE A RAVEN

That looks after me.

He caws a certain way
    when there are
        coyotes about.

He circles over my
    head as I walk
        down the path.

He is always on the
    watch for me.

I wish that I knew
    his language
        so that I could

Figure out what
    he is saying
        to me.

Why is he so loyal?

He is like a watchdog
    who owns the
        place.

This is not just his home—

He is looking after me.

THE RANCH IS TEEMING WITH BIRDSONG

And the scolding
    of a raven
        on a branch.

How can we possibly
    say that if we
        weren't here
            to hear

There would be
    no sound?

I let the sounds
    tell me

"That idea is all
    wrong."

I APPRECIATE
THE SMELL

Of my own coffee,
    of a single little
        sausage
            rolling

With the heat of the
    pan;

The sound as I
    beat an egg,

Or of the knife
    on the cutting
        board

As I cut up a small
    mushroom
        to go with it.

When it rained
    my husband
        used to
            say,

"Aren't you glad
    you have
        a roof over
            your head?"

I CAN'T TELL YOU

How good it feels
    in a quiet pause
        before the day
            begins

In thinking of family
    ones far away
        or close

When a glow
    surrounds them
        and makes
            me

Feel they are safe
    no matter
        what they
            are doing.

I HAVE STRONG EVIDENCE

On many days
    that a few moments
        of gratitude and
            love

For the things or ones
    I think of and
        love

Pays off during the
    day in a sense
        of harmony

Throughout the
    day.

I have time now
    to do this

Where in early life
    I had to swing
        my legs out
            of bed

The moment my
    eyes opened

To start the day.

So much of my memory
    and choice of
        thought

Goes back to those
    early days

And winds up on
    them as they
        are today

With blessings for
    the day at
        hand.

CHAPTER VI
TITO, THE WHISTLING
STORYTELLER AND HELPER

TITO IS MY HELPER

If not whistling at work
    he is telling me
        stories

While driving me
    to town

Or leaning on a
    shovel or
        holding a broom.

TITO

Lives in Chupadero.

One morning when driving
    me into town

He said, "I bought
    myself another
        car."

"Tito," I said, "You are
    a born car
        lover.

What did you want
    another car
        for?

Are you going to
    fix it up?"

"It is a classic,
    a 1970 Monte Carlo
        Chevrolet.

It is all clean,

No rust,

No dents,
    and the original
        paint job,

And I got it running."

"Are you going to
  sell it?"

"No, I am going
    to keep it
      for my wife."

I shook my head
    and
        laughed.

"I got it for a thousand
    dollars," he said.

Two days later,
    he said,

"You know the car
    I got?"

"Yes," I said.

"I found a lawn mower
    in the trunk.

When I saw my friend
    who sold me the
        car

I asked him,
    'You want to buy
        a lawn mower?

I have a good one
    I'll sell you
        for ten
            dollars.'

'No,' he said, 'I have
    a lawn
        mower,

It is in the shed.'

When he looked it
    wasn't there.

He asked his wife,

'Where is my lawn mower?'

'You ought to know,
    you put it in the
        trunk of
            the old
                car.'"

THE SAME MORNING

Tito had another joke.

"I went to the casino
      with my friend.

I had fifty dollars.

My friend said,
      'Loan me the
          fifty dollars;
            I want to
                play.'

I loaned him the
      fifty.

'I bet you a case
      of Cokes

Against a case of
      beer you
          will lose,'
            I told him.

And I got the case
      of beer."

Another time—

"I had a hundred
      dollars.

I went to the cashier.

'Give me five
      five dollar
          winning
              throws.'

And I played
      and lost.

I changed my
      money into
          quarters.

I had a tap on
      my shoulder.

It was my job
      supervisor.

He said, 'Loan me
      your quarters

And I'll play for both.'

He played and won
      two hundred thousand."

"Then did he split
      with you?"
          I asked.

"He gave me back
      what I loaned
          him."

"Tito!" I said,
  but he just
    laughed

And said, "We are good
  friends."

Stretching the amount
  of the winning
    was just a part
      of the joke,
        I knew.

WHEN I FOUND THAT TITO WAS A GOOD DRIVER

I had him drive
  me in my Scout.

I still sat up front.

He drives exactly as
  I used to drive

Going straight to where
  we were to go.

He has been here
  all his life

And knows more
  short cuts to
    get there

Than I ever knew,
  that are not as straight
    but shorter.

I see places
  that I never
    saw before

And people recognize
  him and honk
    at us all over
      town.

He takes me to Market
  and helps me
    find things
      on the
        shelves.

WHEN TITO FIRST STARTED TO DRIVE FOR ME

I rode with him
    in his truck.

The doctor I was to see
    crossed the street
        with a cup of coffee
            in his hands.

When I got to his office
    he said, "Did I see
        you getting out
            of an old yellow
                truck ?"

"That was me,"
    I said.

"Well, I have one just
    like it that I
        drive to the office.

My children are
    embarrassed

About me parking
    it next and
        in between

Other doctors' cars
    but I love
        my old
            truck.

I carry fertilizer in it
    for my flower
        beds

And my friends are
    always borrowing
        it."

"Well," I laughed—

"I used to see Georgia O'Keeffe
    come to town for
        groceries

And she was sitting
    up front with
        her driver

Of an old truck.

If she could do it,
    I could do it

And if I can do it,
    you can do
        it.

But I would have
    done it
        anyway."

I AM ALWAYS
SCOLDING TITO

For loaning his
    good tools
        to his friends,

Who never bring
    them back.

"You know the tools
    I told you about
        that I loaned
            my neighbor?

I went yesterday
    and got them
        back—"

A year later.

ON ONE DAY

Tito and his brother
    went out to clean
        my irrigation
           ditches,

And were back
    at my house
        shortly.

I had a visitor
    and excused
        myself.

Tito was standing by
    his truck
        sullen and
           mad.

"What's the matter?"
    I asked.

"I am never going
    to work for you
        anymore."

"Ah, come now,
    what's wrong?"

"You wanted Lino
    and me to
        clean your
           ditches.

And Ramon has
    cleaned them."

"I didn't tell Ramon
    to clean the
        ditches.

He was just supposed
    to clean the
        yard."

Tito got in his truck
    and left.

My friend said,
    "Oh, I am so
        sorry."

"He will be back,"
    I said.

The next morning
    he was back as
        though nothing
            happened.

Ramon said, "I didn't
    know,

I thought you wanted
    me to clean
        everything."

"Don't worry," I said.

"I'll just have to be
    more careful."

These two speak
    together when
        they have
            to,

Each doing their
    own separate
        jobs.

Lino, Tito's brother,
    said nothing
        of the affair.

I've known him
    since he was
        a boy of
            ten.

I COULDN'T FIND A SHOE

I looked everywhere
    for it, come spring,

When I no longer
    wanted to wear
      my boots.

Tito came bringing
    my laundry
      from his wife.

I said, "Tito, I can't
    find the mate
      to this little
        shoe."

I showed him—

And he got the ladder
    and looked in
      a high cupboard

Where it should
    or could possibly
      be.

He said, "There are some
    brown shoes,
      some sandals,

Some sheepskins,
    but I don't see

The shoe you are
    looking for.

Have you looked
    under your
      bed?"

The next morning
    I got out my
      broom,

Threw the long overhanging
    bedcovers up,

Got down on my knees—
    and looked.

There was a large painting
    stored there,
      a mousetrap,
        some Kleenex,

And something else
    under the far side
      of the bed.

I went around—
    got down on my knees
      again

Swept the broom under
    and sure enough
      there was my
      shoe.

I called his number
    and a grandson
      called him in
        from watering
          his horse.

"Tito," I said, "You did
    it again.

I found my shoe
    under the bed."

CHAPTER VII
OF HOME, FAMILY AND FRIENDS

FAMILY AND FRIENDS

Come only once in
    a while.

The rest of the time
    I have to myself

To just think
    of the rest of
       the world—

Of the people
    and animals
       in it,

Of the days and
    nights we
       share,

Of the haunts we
    like,

Of painters and
    paintings,

Of historians and poets,

Of shepherds
    and of dogs and
       goats,

Of strains of flute
    or jazz band.

Or quiet rivers
    and giant floods,

Of fires and Indian
    drums;

Memory switching
    from one place
       to the other

With no time
    in between,

While the fire on
    the stove
       burns the

Stuff in my pot!

SOMETIMES

My house is
    like Grand
        Central Station

With friends or
    family dropping
    in.

Sometimes I don't
    see or talk to
        anyone for
            days.

MY HOUSE

Is like a hermitage—

Not in the woods
    but where the
        cars pass by.

Not connected
    to any church
        or formalized
            organization

Or already
    standardized
        thought

But a place where
    past thoughts
        come to now.

In a timeless time
    when I sit after
        breakfast

With my elbows
    on the table

And my chin
    in hands.

And think,
    "What now?"
        Though

I may have been
    up in the night
        or the wee hours
            of the morning

Writing.

I AM GLAD

For all memories

And for all the
    conveniences
      of today,

For family and friends:

For tiny feet that
    patter from
      one end of the
        house

To the other
    the minute they
      arrive

From wherever
    they have
      been.

I used to go to
    them.

I saw them arrive
    when put in
      their cradle,

And now they come
    to me and
      bring their
        children

To Great Myrtle's
    house!

WHEN THEY COME

They are free
    to roam my
      twenty acres

Cross the fence
    and play in
      the shallows
        of the river

They come back
    muddy, cold
      and wet;

Dry off and go
    out again;
      find the horse

And feed him
    carrots

Or go in the house
    and watch TV
      for hours.

Fathers and mothers
    doing their thing,
      or just hanging
      out

Doing nothing—

Resting and feeling
    the peace of
      the house. . .

Or cooking!

WHEN I WAS SMALL

I awoke

On winter
   mornings to
      a faint light

Coming from the
   kitchen

And a faint flickering
   from a wood
      stove

Where I was to
   stand and
      put on my
         clothes

In the living room
   a few steps
      from my
         bed.

I do the same things
   in my own house.

I mean about
   the light—

One in the kitchen
   where I feed
      my dog

And put on some
   oats and

Plug in my coffee,

Then turn on a
   light at the
      end of my
         table

In the living room—

And that is it.

The rest of the house
   is in semi-
      darkness

Just as it was
   when I was a
      child.

I love it.

OTHER CHILDHOOD MEMORIES

Come with that
    soft dim light
        of the early
            morning:

My dad stropping
    his long bladed
        razor

On the strop that
    he threatened
        to spank us
            with

If we weren't good
    children.

It hung in the kitchen
    beside the small
        mirror

Above the wash pan
    we all used

Before we had an
    indoor bathroom,

Which wasn't
    too long ago.

ANOTHER THING DURING CHILDHOOD

That woke the whole
    household

Was the smell of
    baking biscuits
        and ham

Cooking on my mother's
    wood-burning
        stove

And the thought of
    cream gravy
        to go with it

And a cup of hot
    chocolate—
        or coffee,

The sound of the streetcar
    bumping over the
        railroad tracks,

And the flutter of
    coats, boots and
        hats,

A lunch
    our mother
        put in our hand
            at the door,

And her kiss
    as we fled to
        catch the car
            for school.

AT SCHOOL

My first grade
 teacher told
  us—

The difference
 between people
  and animals

Is that we can
 think and
  animals
   can't.

I was ready to
 leave my
  books

And go home;

To apologize to
 all the animals
  I knew,

And never go
 back to school.

WE DID IT

For Wilfred and Edith

When the time was
   right;

Piled our things
   into the wagons

And drove up to
   your place;

Lit the fire,
   unpacked the
      cars

And all scattered
   here and there

To do their thing.

Fantastic memories
   of deer and elk;

Horses in the barn,
   heavy boots
      and coats;

Dogs aglee
   and cats;

Mountains covered
   with snow and
      gleaming in
         golden light;

Christmas tree
   dragged in and
      put on stand,

Tinsel all around
   and tons of presents—

Time out for drinks
   and a bite to
      eat;

The sun went down
   and evening put
      us all together.

It was Christmas Eve
   and all was
      well.

In vivid memory,
   I am transported
      there

To unwrap this gift
   from you

And give you
   thanks for my
      being there,

With you and all
   of the family.

Lovingly,
   your Mom
      and mother-in-law.

TOM AND MARION

Lived in the
    big city

Where one building
    could cover several
        blocks.

I always went
    when they would
        call

And so would
    their other mother-
        in-law

And other members
    of their family.

They were great
    on family
        get-togethers

And never worried
    about having
        to step over

Or around suitcases
    or sleeping bodies
        here and there,

At their home
    or at their
        children's,

Or at mine.

TOM AND HIS WIFE

Had three girls;

The three girls each
        wonderful
                husbands

And they each
        two children
        and one

Borrowed from China.

Wilfred and Edith
        had three children
                a girl and two
                        sons.

Out of that
        came a good
                husband

For one, and a good
        wife for another
                and six children,

Making all-together
        twelve great
                grandchildren

And a thirteenth
        from China for
                Myrtle

And beautiful
        memories of the
                lone son.

MY MEMORY

Rolls back to the
        very beginning
                of my life

And pictures perfectly
        everything.

I marvel at this
        most wonderful
                thing,

Of how we can see
        everything

Which is only a memory:

And how quickly
        it all comes
                back to life —

In the middle
        of washing
                dishes

Or making
        my bed,

Or sitting at
        my drawing
                board.

AND IF I HAD IT

To do over again
  I would stop what-
    ever I am
      doing

Around four o'clock
  and give my
    husband

That cup of tea
  and some
    crumpets

That he often wished
  for as brought
    up

By a mother who
  did that for
    her husband.

Or like he was used
  to from a maid in
    the basement
      kitchen

Of a three or four
  story house
    in England

When he had four
  brothers and a sister —

To share it with.

IN MY FIRST HOUSE

Of my married
  life

We ate in the kitchen
  on a small
    cherry wood
      table,

Or on our lap,
  buffet style,
    when we had
      company.

Now if I were
  doing it again

I would take off
  the lamp, books,
    ash trays and
      magazines

And set the beautiful
  long library
    table

And bring up the
  chairs

As I do here
  for guests in
    my living
      room.

WHEN WE EAT FOOD

With the pleasure
    of eating

The very atmosphere
    of pleasure
        is full of energy.

More energy comes
    from the pleasure
        of eating

Than it does from
    the food.

Food gets its energy
    from the atmosphere.

We might ask
    what is the
        atmosphere

In which we are eating:
    Is it pure cosmic
        energy?

Or is it full of worry
    and strife?

We can do a lot
    to cleanse the air
        just by our
            own thinking.

The best cleanser
    is the appreciation
        of cosmic
            energy:

Of the beauty of anything
    or anybody you
        can see beauty
            in:

Of all the things you
    think of as a little
        more than just
            acceptable.

If the one in your
    mind or before
        you

Is a friend or, best of
    all, loved

The atmosphere
    is charged
        with energy,

And food for thought.

"GOOD MORNING"

I said to my
    neighbor one morning,

"Did your daughter
    leave for her
        home today?"

"Yes, she got off
    to an early
        start."

"I am glad that
    you gave me
        a chance

To meet her—

She is a lovely woman.

I know that you
    and your husband loved
        to have her come."

"He didn't know
    who she was,

And when I got in
    bed with him
        last night

He said, 'Do I know
    you?'"

She was laughing
    and I laughed
        too.

MY SIDEKICK BROUGHT ME

My mail
   so that I wouldn't
      have to cross
         the highway.

I met her at her
   car one day.

She had her dark
   glasses on
      though it was
         getting pretty
            late.

I had come out
   to take my last
      evening walk
         with my
            dog.

So she walked down
   the drive with me
   with her dog.

"Arilia had to put her
   dog down last
      night.

She didn't get home
   until after three A.M."

I asked, "What doctor
   did she take the
      dog to at night?"

"To the clinic which
   is open all
      night."

"Liza said it had
   a tumor on its
      heart."

"Liza?
   You said, Arilia."

"I said Liza—

You better get
   a hearing
      aid," she said.

"You better get your
   names straight."

"How is your new
   hearing aid?" I asked.

"The sound is all right,
   but I can't always
      understand.

I have to get used
   to it."

I watched until she
   drove across
      the road

And said thanks
    to her guardian
        angel.

Then I went in with
    my dog

And closed the door
    for the night.

Thoughts of her
    came in with
        me;

Always offering to
    do something
        helpful

Staying overnight
    when I was ill,

Calling from town,
    "Do you need
        something?"

I laughed when she
    locked herself out
        of her car

Which gave me
    something to
        do for her

Or when she calls
    and asks, "Who
        shall I call—

My john's stopped up?"

Our evening walks
    with our dogs
        I would sorely
           miss

If she were not
    just across the
        street.

She has been to
    Europe sixteen
        times,

Asking me to go
    with her once
        or twice.

But I was always
    preparing for an
        art show

Building a house
    or writing a
        book.

She owns a house
    I designed and built
        forty-seven years
           ago

And lives in it with
    her grand piano,
        Indian rugs
        and

Her schnauzer dog,

Which could not be more
    pleasing to me.

STED TOLD ME

Years ago,
   "You are one
      in ten thousand,"

Brightening days
   when I couldn't
     hear him
       say that.

I like my home,

I like the silence,

I've done and had
   everything.

There is a story
   and a remembrance

Of every door hung,

And every screw
   put into
      place.

I sometimes change
   things to suit
     myself

But that is no different
   than it always
     was.

I never lose anything
   of beauty that
     he made.

I just add my touch,
   like when I flagstoned
     the broom-swept
       patio

Where he
   loved to sit

To watch the stars
   in back of our long,
     stretched-out house.

WHEN I HAD HIM

I slept like a babe.

While night after night
   he didn't sleep
      a wink.

In the morning
   I would get up

All bright-eyed and
   bushy-tailed

With a new idea
   of what we
      should do.

He would protest—

"You keep springing
   these ideas
      on me."

But the idea
   was already
      implanted

And nearly always
   carried out.

THE SEPARATION OF

Husbands and
   wives cannot

Quell these two.

We only find how
   Universal Love
      is as Companionable
      Mind.

Love is our primary
   base of intelligence
      for the bee,

The blade of grass,
   and for every
      potential for

Further possibilities.

BEING OPPOSITES

We are attracted
    to one another

But when we are
    together there
        is a sense

Of being mine;

He is mine
  or
      she is mine.

And we start
    wanting mine

To start acting
    as mine

Which takes away
    the sense of
        being ourselves;

We foolishly don't
    see what we are
        doing to one
            another,

And begin to blame
    him or her

For all kinds of things.

Mistrust and con-
    fusion sets
        in

And we back
    away from
        union.

Or grin and bear
    it because
      we have
          made a
               commitment.

Commitments
    are broken
        right and
          left.

And we make the
    same mistake
        with another

And another and
    another

Until we see our
    mistake;

Or we keep a commitment
    and finally learn
        to appreciate
          the other

As other

And a complement
    to ourselves.

And love again
    and become one

As in the beginning.

NO HOUSE IS BIG ENOUGH

To house two women
    and a male
        unless

One woman is
    big enough to say,

"Give him to the
    other."

If it is ruled by a
    Magistrate,

"Cut him in two."

If that one who says,
    "Give him to
        the other,"

Is his mother, she
    not only loves him
        but is wise,

If this one is the one
    he is mating.

Mating caused the other
    long ago to
        deliver him.

MY UPS

Are in both—

Having a house
   full,

And in the silence
   when alone.

I am grateful
   that there have
      been no disconnections
         in our family.

CHAPTER VIII
THEN AND NOW

GOOD MORNING, TOM

Tell me the truth—
   can you see?

If the Mind is all
   seeing how
      could it be

That you not
   see?

Can I help you
   there if you

Are under the
   impression

That you can
   not see?

Let us be free
   of all wrong
      notions;

See wrong teachings
   which tie
      us down.

What is pure
   and simple
      truth

Which I should
   know

And so could you
   if truth is
      true

And truth is truth
   everywhere?

Are you with me
   when in my
      mind?

If so, then you
   are here

And there are no
   boundaries
      between us.

No restrictions
   for who can
      see

And who not
   see.

I believe you are
   aware of
      all that
         is here;

Not just tucked
   away in your
      memory

But with me
   still.

Do you have
   something
      to say,
         Tom?

Can you see—

I've been thinking
   about your saying
      that you wish

That you could see
   your daughters
    and how they
      have grown.

It is a natural thing
   that you might
     think that you
      can't see.

Because you don't
   anymore
     have physical
      eyes.

But that is a mistake
   easily made
     yet surprising.

One is apt to think of
   one in spirit of
     knowing everything;

But not so.

We who are still in
   physical shape
     are the shape
      of spirit.

We are spirit in
   physical form

And it is the spirit
   that sees.

In spirit is all
   cognitive ability.

Or the lack of it.

I think you only
   lack the knowledge
     that you can
      see.

STED SAID

We will be together
    again

And there has been
    a lot of evidence
        that

He never went
    anywhere

And is still here.

If we are both spirit
    made evident
        or unmade

What is our difficulty;

What is the language
    or the silence

Which would allow
    us to communicate?

There is a sense
    that is missing

But if there is a sense
    that is missing

I want to find it!

I am open to it.

It must come.

It is here,
    but where?

Everything is first
    in spirit unformed
        until

Called out.

I am calling for it
    now,

To take a form
    of consciousness

So that I will know
    it for what
        it is—

Spirit in a form
    that eyes can
        see

And understand,
    and can truly say,
        "I see."

HOW CAN WE KNOW

What death is
    without experiencing
        it

Or paying attention
    to others who
        have?

Just knowing
    that others
        have

Should make us
    open to the
        fact

And that is all
    we need

In order to stave
    off the experience

And turn our thoughts
    to other things
        beyond what

That experience
    has in hold.

We set our own
    time for
        things.

And it is always
    time to go
        beyond where
            we are.

We have our eyes
    in front of our
        head

For this very purpose.

DEAR STED

You were besieged
   by the idea
      that I would

Fall in love with
   someone
      else.

If you only knew
   how much
      I still love
         you!

I suppose it was
   right for
      the time.

You told me,
   "Take care
      or else."

And this made
   me more
      determined.

You heckled
   me, tried me
      in every way
         possible.

Once I said to you,
   "You must
      think that
         I am

The most awful
   person you
      ever knew."

And what was your
   response?

You said, "No, you
   are the best
      person I ever
         knew."

"Then why are you
   always picking
      on me?"

You had no answer
   to that.

But I remember
   so many lovely
      things you said
         and did.

If you have a
   soul, you
      must know

What I am thinking
   now.

I HAD A DREAM

I was lying on the
    bed—

Sted was with me
    and there was
        someone else

In the room.

Sted said to the
    other,

"You can go on,
    I am sleeping
        with Myrtle
            tonight."

I turned over toward
    him

And hugged him
    to me
        and said,

"You are sleeping
    with Myrtle
        tonight."

All I could see
    was his right
        eye

And I never saw
    anything
        more clearly.

It was wide open
    and very large
        and blue.

And I awoke
    and lay there
        thinking,

There is more to life
    than what we
        ordinarily
            see,

And wanting desperately
    to know.

IF I WOULD SAY SOMETHING

My husband never,
ever heard
anyone say,

He would say to me,
"Show that to me
in print."

And the older and
wiser I became
the more often
this would
happen

Which would
annoy him
no end.

But there is a line
in the Bible
which says,

"No man telleth this
to thee."

I always took this to
mean that there
is information
out there

Beyond man's present
knowledge.

And it is certainly
true that we
don't know
everything,

But can get flashes
of this intuitively
as we have a
need.

I needed this intuition, but
he didn't.

He was a very factual
person.

"Show me that in
print."

And he knew far more
printed matter
than I knew.

I was very aware
of that, which
made me

More intuitive
in trying to keep
abreast of what

He knew, but he
took it as a
threat

To almost the very
end of his
life,

When truly we became
man and wife.

And it is for myself,
for him and
others like
ourselves

That I have for years
been putting things
in print.

But for him, I don't
think I would have
ever written
a thing.

Painting would have
been my sole means
of expression.

And I would have
missed a richness
of understanding

Of what it was that
I was feeling about
life and my
surroundings.

That is why he is
ever in my
mind

Though I am
alone
with

Writing my means
of sharing and
caring.

LOOKING BACK

It is no wonder
  that Sted told
    a channeler,

"I was afraid of
    Myrtle's ideas
      years ago."

He was standing
    beside me
      in the kitchen

When boiling fat
  in a skillet
    popped
      out

Onto my arm.

I didn't flinch,
    didn't scream
      or do anything.

He said, "I saw that!"

But he didn't offer
    anything.

He knew that I
    was somehow
      fortified

Against that hot
    grease doing
      me harm.

Another time,
    but I am not
        sure that
            he saw

My shoe, or that
    the soft top
        was cleaved
            in two

By an ax I was
    using—

Or know that
    for a second
        I thought my
            foot was
                cut

But I went on
    finishing my
        job,

Because I sensed
    that "sense of
        foot intact,"

My big toe on one
    side of the cut
        and the second
            toe

On the other side, both
    untouched.

He was a practical
    man—

Believing only in
    what you could
        see, smell and
            touch.

But this he could
    not believe

Though he saw the one
    and could have seen
        the other
            had he been
            there.

WE ARE A HARD

Coffee drinking people;

An impatient and
    thoughtless people;

A highly critical people.

Those who can't take
    it are just out
        of luck.

It is making us all
    tough skinned.

We will all get to be
    like crabs

With hard shells
    and pinchers

To protect our inner
    self.

Or it just might
    make us more
        compassionate;

More ready to toss
    off the insults

Laugh at the silliness
    or to make
        use

Of what is all in it
    if there is anything
        worthwhile.

It is just no use
    to expect people
        to be sweet

All of the time, so I don't
    hesitate to say that
        I don't mind

Living alone.

It is sometimes easier
    on the nerves.

IT IS TIME THAT WE

believed in
    ourselves

Enough to know
    when to let
        something

Bother us,

And when not.

I HAD A DREAM

Last night
   which told
      me

In a round
   about way
      in the

Manner of
   a dream:

When we have
   done all we
      can

But still have
   scars

And bad times,

We might as
   well say
      to ourselves—

It is time to leave
   it all to the
      new and
         young

Which will be
   ourselves in
      return.

But if we do,
   we might have to
      finish the
         game

In a new name,
   so why not now,

And savor the
   accomplishment.

YOUNGER ONES

Have stepped into
   my shoes
      to do

The things for the
   Community I
      used to
         do.

And, as for designing
   and building
      or preserving
         old houses,

Women of today
   think nothing

Of the things I used
   to do as early as
      the 30's.

I was one of the
   first women,
      if not the
         first,

To have a contractor's
   license in New Mexico.

I was an architect
   for the ones I
      designed and
         built for.

There are historic
   plaques to mark
      some of my
         work,

And a Governor's Award
   for Art and Architecture;

A Mayor's Award for
   Visual Arts and
      Literature;

And Museum awards
   for my painting
      as far back as the
         thirties;

Not to brag but
   just to tell you.

And to remember
   that I don't have
      to do it anymore

Than I want to:

For which, as it is,
   is plenty to
      keep me busy.

AS I JUST SAID

I don't do all

Of the things I
   used to do for
      the Community

Or with it.

But I am remembered
   for the things I
      did

And am treated with
   love and respect.

Two men who worked
   for me when
      building

Adobe houses

Came to me when
   their mother
      died,

And I gave them
   one hundred
      dollars to
         fill a need.

And they said,
   "You are our
      mother now."

The Hispanics are very
   gracious

And their elders
   are looked up to

For their wisdom
   and experience.

It is the same with
   the Indians.

It is an honor
   to be accepted
      in this relationship.

I am bordered on
   three sides
      by the Tesuque
         Pueblo land.

Once I was buying
   some jewelry—

A Governor of the State
   of New Mexico,
      years ago,

Gave the Indians right
   to sell their wares
      under the portal

Of the Palace of the
   Governors.

I ran out of cash
   that day when
      buying.

And I asked if they
        would accept
            a check.

The one I was buying
        from hesitated

But a young Indian
        girl next to her

Said, "She is all right;
        she did the books
            on Adobe
                Architecture."

I've lived among
        the Hispanics and
            the Pueblo Indians

For sixty-five years
        and am devoted
            to this land

And its people,
        Anglos included.

Once a young Hispanic
        asked me how
            old I was—

I told him.

Then he wanted to
        know how long
            I've lived here.

I told him.

And he said, "That makes
        you more native
            than I am."

I always did fit in
        with dark hair,
            eyes and
                skin.

All the people
        I built houses
            for are
                gone:

All the men who
        helped me
            build

Are gone.

But new ones
        fit beautifully
            in

To help me take
        care of things.

I CAN'T SAY

That I grieve
  for the ones
    I knew

Because of the new
  and now.

It is as it was
  with them,

A joy and a pleasure
  every day

With only the
  then and now.

CHAPTER IX
THIS IS WHAT I HAVE FOUND OUT

THIS IS WHAT I HAVE

Found out—

That we are always
    coming or going

In or out of decisive
    decisions we
      make.

The universe provides
    the energy and
      stamina

For whichever way
    we decide to
      go.

ALL OUR FACULTIES

Are of the Mind
    and are as
      permanent
      as the
        Mind.

Mind is the primordial
    stuff, life
      Itself,

And all the evidence
    is in Itself;

It does not tell
    us all It
      knows.

It only tells us
    what we
      need

And are open to.

Mind is a growing
    thing

Ever creative of
    things new.

Its forms are in
    and out of
      our visual
        range.

I HAVE A GREAT REVERENCE

For the Mind
and call it God
out of habit

Though I know that
it has had
other names.

I can just say
we need snow
or rain

And get the feeling
that It has heard

And sure enough
it snows or
rains.

Or I can go along
with a passerby
and agree
with him

"We need rain,"
but nothing
happens.

I can ask
where is my
cane,

After I've looked for
it for half an
hour

And laugh when my
eyes light
right on it.

I WANT

The churches
  to clean up
    their act.

This is Palm Sunday.

I was invited to go
  to church

For a beautiful
  service

And I said, "Nope,
  I don't go to
    church."

I have been to
  a certain
    church,

But every time
  everything
    good about
      it

Was spoiled when
  they read their
    creed.

The spoiling line,

"We are sinners. . ."

I want to scream,
  to fight, to
    yell!

Or quietly tell,

You have put
  the biggest
    blight

On the Apple
  Eve gave Adam to eat,

And that every one
  of us has
    had to
      deal with

Who has ever
  "made love."

Nothing ever came
  to live

Without the making
  of love.

No invention,
  no piece of art work
    no music or architecture,

No little copies
  of the ones who
    love:

No flower,

No little rabbit

Not one thing in the
    universe came
       to life

Without love
    between

An expression
    and its conception.

Human beings are
    the only forms
       of life

I know of that have
    been fed this

Expression, "We are
    sinners,"

Leading to the birth
    of misconception

About the making
    of love,

And what it produces.

The woman in me
    is saying, "I am

Not going to bite
    that apple anymore."

The only way to change
    anything

Is to not give credence
    to blight

Just look for
    perfection

To produce
    perfection

In love itself.

Contemplating on perfection
    would carry the
       perfection
          of universal
             order

Into everything
    that concerns
       us.

So what am I
    doing, complaining
       now?

WE SHOULD BE ABLE

To sluff off old ideas
    of a God in heaven

As easily as the
    body sluffs off
        old cells and

Replaces them with
    new each day.

We could see in this
    replacement the
        orderly perfection

Of how the Mind works
    and see It as the
        thing we worship

And call It God.

We could see this
    order in the
        movements

Of the planets
    and realize we
        are on one

And need to
    pool our efforts
        together

With the whole cosmos.

To attain the sense
    of a cosmic
        mind.

WE ARE SO USED TO

Pushing a button
    to turn a light
        on

That it is hard
    to understand
        that light,

Or knowledge,
    comes by the
        wish for knowledge.

We make a place
    for it in our
        mind.

There is nothing there

And then there is something.

This is how it all
    began—

There was nothing
    and then there
        was something.

This is the basis
    of all things.

All comes from
    two phases
        of Mind.

These two phases
   make the Mind;

They are the Mind.

We have not seen
   creation as

Coming from two.

We have said, "God,
He."

That is why we do
   not understand.

We have not given
   the "She" credit

For giving Him a
   place to be.

We have associated
   Being only with
     "He,"

Whereas "He" could
   not have been
     without a place
       to be—

A mating of Mind to give
   Him form.

Longing provides
   the matrix;

Longing provides
   the beginning of
     everything.

Can one have a longing
   without understanding
     what one longs
       for?

WITH THE MIND

What It is
   there is simply
      no excuse

For having a dull
   or unsuccessful
      life.

NOW

I have set
   my sights
      ahead.

Everything in
   my life
      is perfect

So far as home
   and possessions
      go.

Why should I leave
   it now?

What is out there
   now for me
      to see to it

That it is materialized?

That is what matter
   is—it is spirit
      of intention
         realized.

I've worked for
   years beyond

Just getting things
   and keeping
      things

In repair.

It is all in my books.

WE STABILIZE

Our experiences
    within the
        limits of our
            expectations.

With that in mind
    we should be
        encouraged
            to dream.

The universe is
    expanding

There is no need
    to stand still

Unless we like it
    that way

In the name of sameness
    and stability.

But if that turns
    stale

Take a risk
    on the universe
        to support
            you

In whatever it
    is you want
        to do.

A UNIVERSAL MIND

Would know
    everything
        about everything.

It would also
    know everything
        about nothing.

So when a person
    loses eyesight
        or hearing or
           both,

If they only knew
    they could,

They would tap into
    universal knowing

And not feel cut off
    and useless;

Fall sick and die.

They would be vitally
    more alive.

They could be intuitively
    more informed than
        they would be
           reading a book

Or listening to TV.

And with a far more
    simple and
        direct enlightening.

In the far distant past,
    intuition, hearing
        God talking;

Mind, then and now,
    a cordless
        telephone.

So it can be done
    and the doing
        very interesting,

And far more
    than just a
        pastime.

The more we think
    about it, the
        easier it will
           become

For those who need it
    and want it,

And are willing
    to work at it,
        for the great

Joy and connectedness
of a Universal
Mind.

But it would take
a universal calamity
before most of
us

Would even consider
this.

THERE IS A STORY

About Jacob who was
      asleep in the desert
            with his head on
                  a stone

For a pillow.

In a dream he saw
      in the heavens
            a ladder—

With angels descending
      and ascending.

This is the way
      the Mind
            works.

We can be anywhere
      on the rungs:

We can be close to
      the bottom

With a serious
      problem,

And the problem
      can vanish

If we can see
      ourselves on the
            top rung

Above the problem,
      above all of the
            descending rungs.

CHAPTER X
I TANGLED WITH A GOATSKIN RUG

ONE MONDAY MORNING

I tangled with a
    goatskin rug
        in my hallway,

And was thrown against
    the wall,

And down flat on my
    back onto the
        flagstone floor.

Everything on my
    inside was moving
        back into place.

So I lay there thinking,
    "If they haven't lost
        their moorings,

I'll be all right."

When I got up I
    did all right—

Went to town the next
    day and still
        felt all right.

And I laughed about
    it and told
        a few;

Which brought it
    all back, worse
        than it was before.

Now I know that
    you will think
        that I am stretching
           a point—

And you will remind
    me that it often
        takes a few days

For an injury to be really
    felt,

But in those few days
    how many times do
        we revitalize the
           incident?

We can keep the effects
    effectively active
        for years.

We are a mental construct.

YEARS AGO

I made an error.

I got out of a car,
 ran around
  the back

And into the path
 of an oncoming
  car.

I was picked up
 and onto the
  front fender,

And carried about
 twenty feet

Before the car
 stopped.

They wanted to take
 me to hospital

To have the groin
 of my right
  leg X-rayed

But I had a date
 and ran on
  home to
   keep it.

The thought ran
 through my
  mind,

"If I ever have trouble
 with my right
  leg,

The trouble will be
 in my groin."

After seventy years,
 the groin is
  giving me

Trouble.

Again the suggestion
 came to go to
  hospital.

I made an error
 when I ran
  around the car

And right into the
 oncoming car.

In math if one
 makes a mistake

It, when seen,
 is recognized
  as an error,

And given no further
 account.

It is just crossed
 out.

If we don't cross
    out mistakes
        that are made

They are bound to
    show up
        sooner or
            later.

An error is an
    error

And can be crossed
    out no matter
        when this comes
            to mind.

It is crossed out now

And there is no
    need to go to
        hospital.

A wonderful feeling
    issued in its
        place.

A WEEK AGO

I fell,
    the second time
        in a year,

On a stone floor.

I had gone outside
    for a stick of
        wood.

It was on a chilly
    day.

I hadn't taken
    my cane

Because I needed
    my hands.

I started to go up
    two steps in
        the hall,

Turned to remove
    my dark
        glasses

Which flew across
    the floor
        as I

Landed on my head
    and just as
        quickly

A knot as large as
    a hen's egg

Appeared over my
    left eye.

Before I could
    think what
        happened,

I thought that I
    had broken
        my back.

A finger began to
    swell—

My ring finger
    with mother-of-pearl
        set in
            a ring.

And my thin sharp
    worn wedding
        ring.

Orange blossoms,
    long since
        worn
            off

And as sharp as a
    razor blade.

The mother-of-pearl ring
    a sixteenth of an
        inch thick

And one-eighth inch
    wide in
        silver.

The finger bleeding.

I took it all in
    as I lay there

Completely impregnated
    with the idea
        of "fall!"

Knowing that I
    would have to
        suffer

The consequence.

Rings cut off at the
    hospital emergency
        room

Not that day
    but the next.

Back X-rayed
    and leg.

Four hours at the
    hospital

With gentle and excellent
    care.

Wheeled to the car
    in a chair,

By a friend who
    came to my
        need from the

Beginning and
staycd with
me

This full week for
a head scan and
a heart check.

Food at my place
on the table,

A tuck into bed at
night and
a lift out of
the tub

In the morning.

Brain check
"beautiful" the
radiologist
said,

"No shrinkage,
no damage!"

He checked with the
operator twice

To read again, "age 91."

The hardest part
was getting in
and out of
bed.

Today, a week later,
I made it
with more
ease.

And more under-
standing of
why

It was such
an ordeal.

I had let my fortification
down.

Fortification is what my
writing is all
about.

And why my head scan
showed my brain
to be beautiful!

It has been actively
alert and
alive

To pick up loose
information

And put it all
together,

For all the future
stops that one is
bound to encounter.

AND WHO WAS THE ONE

Who came to my
   rescue but the
      one who said,

"You are a devil."

Three times she helped
   me out of the
      bathtub

Wiped my butt
   with a towel,

Fed me day and night
   for two weeks,

All loving and thoughtful
   of my every need. . .

More than making
   up for the six months
      that she stayed
         with me
            before,

When it was but a
   power struggle
      most of the
         time.

This time she made
   a point in
      saying,

"I love your house."

"I love being here."

And I appreciated
   the opportunity
      to return
         her love.

And but laugh
   at what happened
      before

When she needed
   me and I needed
      her,

But neither of us
   wanted to admit
      it.

Which may be the
   way of all suffering
      and adversity,

Blessings in disguise

Healed only by
   understanding.

JUST TONIGHT

I got the full
impact

Of what I have
written

And really comprehended
what I have
said.

How could it have
taken so long

Or been so spasmodic?

I can see

That the things
I have been
writing

Only illuminate
what all vast
thinkers

And writers have
been saying,

But without all
the mystery
and trappings.

It is plain,
simple,

Basic and
understandable.

It is this:
In seeing the
Spiritual and

The Biological
as one.

EPILOGUE

TWO QUESTIONS

Have been asked
of me since
Sted's death

Fifty years ago.

"Don't you ever
get lonely?"

To that I answer,
"yes and no."

The other—

"Didn't you ever
think of
remarrying?"

The answer to that,
"yes and no."

And I tell them
that I am always
happy when

Others do remarry,

But for me
"no."

And here is why—

We lived and worked
together day and
night,

How many people
can say that
of their marriage?

We were both artists
with the same
love and desires.

And had two wonderful
sons.

Our life was intensely
creative and
many sparks
flew

Both working as
hard as the
other.

When he would
have junked
me,

I said, "I am not
giving up all
I've worked for."

And that was
that!

Once when I would
have gladly left
him

There was no
place for me
to go.

And our two boys
were devastated

And full of stories
from other
boys.

I wrote Sted a
note

Telling him a thing
or two that I
was too choked
to say—

Left for groceries
and cried all
over town

That things would
be alright be-
tween us.

And went home.

He met me at
the door

And gave me
a kiss, built
a fire in the
fireplace

And pulled up a
little bench.

We sat before the
fire

And he asked,
"Do you still
love me?"

And I choked,
"Of course."

He tells a channeler,
"I am always
here

And waiting
for her
to join me."

I am in no hurry
but I'll keep
that date.